The Plague Factory

John Edward
LAWSON

For Jayson, my Dirty South denizens, and the rowdy Brits!

by John Edward Lawson

Published by Raw Dog Screaming Press
Hyattsville, MD

First Paperback Edition

Cover illustration: Keith Wigdor, www.surrealismnow.com
Coverdesign: M. Garrow Bourke
Book design: M. Garrow Bourke

Printed in the United States of America

ISBN: 1-933929-31-6

www.rawdogscreaming.com

Also by John Edward Lawson

Novels

Last Burn in Hell: Director's Cut (Picaresque Book One)

Collections

Discouraging at Best

Pocket Full of Loose Razorblades

Poetry

The Troublesome Amputee

The Horrible

The Scars Are Complimentary

Illustrated Books

A Child's Guide to Death (w/Darin Malfi, Dustin LaValley, and Mark Sullivan)

As Editor

Tempting Disaster

Sick

Of Flesh and Hunger

Acknowledgments

Agency of Expense first appeared in *Tin Lustre Mobile/ Poetic Inhalation*

Alive, Alive-Oh first appeared in *Bewildering Stories*

An Elliptical Love first appeared in *Muse Apprentice Guild*

And the Sickness Issues Forth first appeared in *Muse Apprentice Guild*

Annathematic first appeared in *sidereality*

Beyond the Islands first appeared in *sidereality*

Cable Tab first appeared in *Bewildering Stories*

Cataratchet first appeared in *sidereality*

Chicago Jarman first appeared in *Tin Lustre Mobile/ Poetic Inhalation*

A Conversation from Below first appeared in *Tin Lustre Mobile/Poetic Inhalation*

Cursing About Something Else first appeared in *Tin Lustre Mobile/Poetic Inhalation*

Delicate Repulsive Summer first appeared in *Muse Apprentice Guild*

Deranged Benefactor first appeared in *Tin Lustre Mobile/ Poetic Inhalation*

Fashionable Victim first appeared in *Muse Apprentice Guild*

Gene Splicing first appeared in *Tin Lustre Mobile/ Poetic Inhalation*

Heathens Gathered at the Feast first appeared in *Muse Apprentice Guild*

Histrionic first appeared in *Tin Lustre Mobile/Poetic Inhalation*

Insight Erasure first appeared in *Bewildering Stories*

Love Poem #1968 first appeared in *Bewildering Stories*

Nature vs. Nurture, Final Round first appeared in *Muse*

Apprentice Guild
Ontogeny Recapitulates Philogeny first appeared at *LitKicks*
Planned Cityhood first appeared in *Muse Apprentice Guild*
Probe and Puncture first appeared in *Tin Lustre Mobile/Poetic Inhalation*
Read This Before You Get One Day Balder! first appeared in *Bewildering Stories*
She Just Got Home first appeared in *Tin Lustre Mobile/Poetic Inhalation*
Spilling the Battle first appeared in *Muse Apprentice Guild*
Wedding Night in the Flower Bed first appeared in *Tin Lustre Mobile/Poetic Inhalation*
When Ravished Left Behind first appeared in *Tin Lustre Mobile/Poetic Inhalation*

Table of Contents

Author's Note

The Plague Factory has had a troubled history. It was first picked up by a publisher who went under just a month before the scheduled publication date. Eventually it was released by Skull Vomit Publishing as a free, downloadable PDF; within a year Skull Vomit closed shop and it was picked up by Meat Hook Press. Eventually MHP disappeared and the book has been unavailable for some time.

After the reaction to my debut poetry collection, *The Scars are Complimentary*, I decided to split my horror, literary, and experimental poetry into separate volumes. Thus, *The Horrible* contained only horror, *The Plague Factory* only experimental. After that I decided this approach was nonsense and I'd do things however I wanted, leading to the melting pot—and success—of *The Troublesome Amputee.*

Within this book are works evolved from fits of formless desire; normally, one sets out with something specific in mind when writing, but such was not the case with these poems. They seized me between 2002 and 2005.

Some may be fragmented thought more than poetry, some are constructed from the titles of spam eMail, others have been assembled by splicing together several different articles. Some of the work here is experimental in the extreme, some humorous, some might even be offensive...hopefully you'll find it enjoyable.

John Lawson
Landover Hills, Maryland 2/13/07

Alive, Alive-Oh

The proud cockles wave
from the shoreline disturbing
the dandelion slumber which had settled
over my cauterized consciousness.

[I seem to recall]

Where do you cry when the funny
man in your brain has stopped
laughing?

[waves crashing, hard saliva on dentures]

Don't ever let them see you
sweat, particularly if
they are invertebrates preoccupied
with a singularly nasty fingernail
fetish, and florid ambitions

[tines and melted butter]

to appropriate pernicious sin
swelling in their mucus membranes.

[sounds of teeth gnashing]

Ghosts of extravagance swelter-
swarm, an ephemeral dervish
of culinary vengeance and primordial
stomach aches, at the raw bar.

[sinews dispossessed]
In the hot seat Mr. Muscle squirms
through the torpor induced by the lemon juice
rambling deliriously that he is
not who the specters would
have him be.

[screams silenced by smiling lips]

Solemnly sitting in my corner, celery
sticks and appendix in hand,
I clearly observe their palates,
which are empty, having
been long since pillaged of their jade
taste buds and ruby blossoms,
parched and dark as those violated
Egyptian desert sarcophagi.

Delicate Repulsive Summer

You really shouldn't say such
things if you value the sanctity
of your colon. Wiping your
elaborate iron drool: he always
wants you tiny, like a thousand
cooked, raw breasts. Still under
two. So needy.

You recall her enormous language;
it lathers your vision like those
gorgeous gardens she tends.
Uncle out back at the distillery,
remember? Girlshine worship
shaking the black chain apparatus
of your shadow symphony.

The Bedroom as a Room of Her Own

She sleeps on a bed of males. The soles of her feet bask in the rage of their burning hot goals as she crosses them, one at a time. That's only possible because of her faith heeling, which cost an extra fifty hollars down at the Footwhere Liquidator Cathedral.

He didn't anticipate six months at sea when signing on as a shoe sailsman. Admittedly, it was an improvement over plying mortgages at Moaning Leasers of Paris. As a shoe hustler, though, he only earns a sea minus. Bearing that in mind he puts his sales to the wind.

The captain of industry finds himself troping through the lightfields, his sea legs incompatible with her air legs—fitted with air souls, as they are. Yet even she slips on the stairway to heaven, tumbling like a lead gremlin. The captain sees to it that she is resigned to bed rest; each plank of his suspicion builds a seawall against her surging desires. Indeed, the levy has broken.

Read This Before You Get One Day Balder!

Scene 10: colored with no meaning
Scene 7: didactic aneurisms rule the day
Scene 1: person tells themselves they are "sick"
[for the purpose of amusement]

Scene 5: intermission
Scene 4: Sick Person visits doctor who is not
Nostrodamus

Scene 11: sneezing

Scene 8: Sick Person manages to turn own tongue
into dental floss
[for the purpose of hygiene]
Scene 10: gratuitous snickering
Opening credits: I feel fine

Closing credits: I swear an oath from beyond
the grave [casting call]
Scene 32: Sick Person fails to convince
himself [internalized dialogue
and yes I do believe in mutual exclusivity]

Cabbie Exhaust

Put a gun to the back
disconcerting in a way.
That guy over there needs
a shave if you ask me, ___ regarding
that sort of thing, don't they?
They line up all _____ get paid
by how long they work.

One time somebody pulled up
to talk to me—a muffler cannot
block out all the noise.
The EPA has regulations
which I guess you don't.
No, its not _______ of his ____
fact that he does not
speak English.

Some folks claim ____'s a nut
hair away from all day long
...whats up with that?
Hookers, lawyers, cabbies...they are
hitting her leg man, I'm telling you.
The maintenance facility is
the ________ arteries of the city.

Sometimes he is intimidated
by the head and: blam!
After a while even a friend ______—
and the wheel was right on my foot!
The bumper was just _________;

they are the plaque
blocking up nowhere around here.

The Sexy Zen Buddhist

S
tra
ngely Orthodox
Ballet
Early Actor
Shouts
The Evangelical
Brow
Evangelical Is Early.

Shows
to
a consciousnes
s s
and
prays despairingly no
is
e
les
s
ly, s
tra
ngely
egocentric
programmable
orthodox ballet
early
actor
shouts
the evangelical

brow
evangelical
is
early
waiter
popu
la
tes
busily brut
ally,
voluntarily, rhythmic
ally that
waiter

is
sex
y
Zen Buddh
is
t
bawls softly
clinic
ally,
enticingly
numb
ly
Look!
A
rhythmic king cros
s

hug

s kindly
quick

unprincipled
be
auti
ful fatal
is
tic ne
w
cros
s musician
jangles
subtly
easily, rapidly, afterward
Ah!
A young pr
is
oner
weak
Buddh
is
t occludes
the
weak
girl
is

the Buddh
is
t
cinematic?

Histrionic

SYMPTOMS:

A pervasive pattern I could do without, and for attention seeking, the area around adulthood is present in a variety of contexts, as indicated with his tongue by the following:

(1) is uncomfortable to fail; he or she is not the center of attention. Isn't this hair—to be more intimate—totally insane? My red skirt SUCTION men can just AROMANTIC when peeking out from water-fish-shark. How do you mean COVEN is often characterized OF a bodacious booby shirt? [it's all about me].

(2) interaction with others leads subject to style in WHAT like so, by inappropriate sexual nights and well-scored behavior, one can't remember what DEMAND AN ANSWER. Actually, I go lacking an appearance any time I draw. Yo man, check ONE and [exaggerated gestures] was mackin' that joint last SUCTION of thirteen phone numbers?

(3) VIRGIN displays rapidly shifting classes like my bodacious emotions CORRELATION is my favorite; ONE I know this for a fact: every one of the water-blue-sky shallow expressions like "Is it possible to begin early up in management" will be on the quiz DISORDER. And examinations. I want to ACTION all, I'm just OF sick! SOMETHING IS WRONG.

(4) consistently uses physical attention to COVEN self, but hides airplane-holiday and so on under "it." He said "Are there tests that are seductive or provocative in bed with..." That's what I can do! The most unhappy creation of all is FORCED VIRGINITY.

(5) has a style defined by "PRIESTESS" and now is excessively

impressionistic in anger, every detailed time; oh, I'm not an appropriate DISORDER? You know what ACTION I mean?

(6) shows self-dramatization. HISTRIONIC you behave too theatrically, and the expression of emotion in you just screams and screams. Yeah, but if easily influenced by my tongue you'd leave her for me, right? What does it see: my tush, a guy puts a cherry in his mouth—five or more in a knot—and gives it to you? What do I know, I'm in situations in which I in love this PERSONALITY!

(7) is suggestible, i.e., a virgin in all others or circumstances that SUCTION off the honeys. What's that called, the out OF control nipples? I know that's ACTION their song. ONE called it. Listen, it's cool about musicians PRIESTESS knowing that damn-it-attack-blood ties the stem [not an appropriate IM subject between friends].

(8) AUREOLES affirms that relationships "Scantron" it out…then, they actually are about me. No, I'm not exhibiting OF excessive emotionality "again"…think mine look [laughs as if joking]? Not bad, eh? Good enough to steal INSANE.

Somnambulance Sirens at 3 a.m.

When mutilation comes knocking, will you want
to answer? I watched money change hands
into claws, into legal footnotes tearing
at the flesh of morality. She work at,
how you say, "T-T bar"—because she is having
knockers. Her warm encirclement still
resonates on my tatters, my organic flags
flapping in society's gusts of hot air. The yearning is
a herald, the vibrations of footfalls yet to be
marched. Your intuition is familiar with this
one, yes? Fellini's murderer creeping up on
you from the burnt end of the spectrum,
his nose marred by proxy.

Jarrgantuan RamPager

midnight rotten gunmetal gums
pain-filled Sagittarius shores bury my mind
my harm is safe for tonight
your baby is my jiggling bait in this worsening darkness
just as wrong as your fields are barren

this laugh signifies another heart attack

fevered mastication of broken joints and cracked
organs tasting velvet-contagious
force my sin to fold in on itself,
one of those rabbinical concubines
going down like some misbegotten
juggernaut traversing facile cityscapes

concrete operational unreasoning crumbling

a poor man's decay is a rich man's flimflam
this language of rotten molars
creates leviathans even greed cannot
tame with sanitary intent or break
through seasons of smiling distemper

it's all a slobber-burning barn-knocker in the end

Patriots Appreciate Spicy Food

Sometimes those old people
will beat the stuffing out
of a turkey. Yankee Doodle
called that "spaghetti."

When you find lobsters in your
mailbox, or the cheese sauce in
your hip pocket, Yankee Doodle
categorized that as "spontaneous lasagna."

Voyeuristic carnivores armed
with binocular tongues watch old men
scrubbing their corns. Yankee Doodle
labeled that "baked ziti."

Amefist and Quartz

1.) ABSTRUSIFY

Biased aesthetic money
(athiest risable) one jam?

The crazy complication: an egotistical despot had the Internet
in a sow's ear *lovely in the dark*

how is the demon of [blank thought]
them, are everlasting eternal dead cliches
like at least
(dark inertia) one jam?

The philosopher kisses. The philosopher indulges.

A frenzy of

...

Them are not
Madonna I am too
many of [blank thought] ambiguity I will be;
worshipped. The explorable bikini moves
from a Zen moment,
extends from your unborn descendant: it never overhears

(shut up now!)

Most bureaucracies callously and amiably walk
to an appointment which is

—did I mention that I am an interracial
mongrel?! The product of bang?!
Interbang?!

—is like my ****. It never overhears
most bureaucracies callously

[scarred ear wax] and so burns an atlas [lose your way to
the stake in your heart,
it will find you anyway in a perfect world]

to change these difficult times, I'd pray
for support from this week's movie star. Too many
of your guardian angels are dissimilar to brutality
on the nude channel. She throws brutality
to the cannibalistic groom

—to your celestial body my darkness is a meteorite—

her hunk is similar to an archetypal love? I have failed
to find an arch anywhere
in "love."

The suffocating fresh slithers from
controversy strangely comes to her hunk,
an appointment is rotted. *Burn*
your atlas, a calendar is summer's last
tragedy, empty the chamber
and pull the trigger.

A famous politician's memory.

Reefs gather in flavorless boss crowds, smoking
horse ****** and burning atlases to become
increasingly drunk;
atlas to the shore, atlas to
your home, your last memory,
explain things to an oaf.

She hurries to particular chimpanzees as his distress
is palpable. Sway.

If at least one nerd had the explorable
bikini your *** ****** would be rotted.
A cannibalistic groom is similar to these difficult
times. I'd demand that groom is like Love.

It postpones joyfully…
Your unborn descendant: it eviscerates joyfully…

An eager consequence longs for support
from the nudity, the atlas, from the
atlas,
with the atlas we are now without;
it desires the altas' ashes!

The philosopher kisses. A corpulent
victim is his partner.
A deranged wife practices modern failure
while everlasting eternal dead cliches—
like your unexpressed love—long for procreations
to brutality on the Internet [how
is today's television viewing audience?].

It helps us echo.
Cheap, aesthetic money
[blank thought] *one jam?*

The philosopher kisses. A frenzy
of ambiguity [I will be worshipped].

The moral majority? That groom
makes connections to the moral
majority! Because cliches sleuth.
Amefist and quartz
        help us echo.
Cheap, aesthetic money
        one despairs a false poet.
That groom makes connections
        to keep tasty. This young
woman shows the desire, your future
        spouse is actually a brilliant
hidden atheist, a little-appreciated
        joy of a frenzy, of ascendencies
a lurid [blank thought]!

Your mania to consume: anxious,
erroneous! It's 49 percent sure
that groom is similar to increasingly drunk atlases,
to a Zen moment (extended).

2.) WILLFULLNESS

A memory. A coral reefer, flavorless in your lungs, reminding you of subaquatic shimmering exiles which dreamt by last week. Smoking horse, amiably walk to the cancerous mass of your unborn descendant: it

never overhears callously (and quartz shows an eager consequence from the loins of this week's movie star). Too many. I am too. "People is so rotted." A risk: a wide audience helps us make sense of a false support from the suffocating desire, a frozen moment, an amiable disagreement which ends in metallic penetration. Consumptives are going to make it into the White House this year, or so I hear. Evolution! A cannibalistic groom is today's television viewing audience. An authentic human being is actually
the demon and quartz, rotted, bizarre, a naked consumption—erroneous!

[blank thought]

3.) SALVATION IS GRAND

It's 99 percent sure that pet rock is
the variable explorable bikini
[the evolutions subscribe to her
auburn attraction…]

Some of us make sense of ambiguity,
I will be the person—erroneous!

It's 49 percent sure
It's 19 percent sure
It's 77 percent sure
It's 91 percent sure
It's 54 percent sure It's [blank thought] percent sure It's 9 percent sure It's a-hell-of-a-big-number-percent sure It's 84 percent sure It's 74 percent sure It's 100 percent sure:

Brutality!

A formless psychologist—the copilot's
drowsy captive—ends a deranged wife,
masters modern failure while a hunk
[*why are everlasting eternal dead*
cliches the moral majority?]

"Early babies crucify art."
As has been proven! By archeologists
who bore children late in life with
chisels, masterfully decietful, longing for support
while burning a br[abnormal atlas]a.
A deranged modern failure is an egotistical
CREATURE WITHOUT LAXATIVES
and translucent explorable bikinis are
endorsed from this week's movie star's armpit.
Too many tiny advertisers fit in there—
erroneous!

It's 49 percent sure that early babies are
your mania, are her hunk, are an oaf, are "she,"
are dencreasingly drunk and an atlas,
...are being kissed mercilessly by the philosopher
to change these difficult times.

I would pay half a mind for organized kind
air: angry excitement/awful white/joyful
glowing/avant-garde/denial/the suffocating
/fresh controversy. Strangers come to keep tasty.

"Young woman flashes her dutiful, abnormal abstinence."
My friend = I simply pretend to feel molested by your words.

Annathematic

when it grows inscrutably cold she will prance,
unfathomably cold it is not a party
to the crime—not the heat
of passion to be blamed this time, nor praised,
lauded, cheered and carried about the anteroom
of the slaughterhouse—she's dancing
with bemused skin flapping (her body's
dry-rotted drapery; moth-worn and sun-spoilt,
wretchedly cute in the utter lack
of energy, ambient or otherwise) to inflict
blows or more to the point massive head
trauma on the blades.

damn the blades with their inflexible handles
and implacable reflections of transparencies,
gossamer realities floating by on a frosted breath
hoping that Old Mister Saber will finally kick
the bucket this year so the precious rump
roast may be had, slow-rusted and basted
in its own nefarious molten juices under
a rainbow eye and a thunder-perfect monobrow…
the costume ball at the inauspicious end
of nothing continues uninterrupted.

Ontogeny Recapitulates Phylogeny

A detective named Matilda is lost in a box. Sherlock Holmes is dispatched to rescue her but he couldn't fight his way out of a wet paper bag with his face on fire. Overcooked and soggy he returns with his head hung in shame, defeated.

But Watson refuses to lose his feet—the shoes alone cost him a fortune. However, he becomes mystified by pots full of hair and their magical allure, and is made forgetful of his quest. A box is sent to cover the pots, but cannot complete the task because it is already full—the little girl inside seems to be stuck.

A rat named Nicodemus observes it all, laughing from the shadows. He returns to his new home, the recently vacated feet of Sherlock Holmes. Matilda finally sets a fire to escape her imprisonment but Encyclopedia Brown—ever the good samaritan—douses the flames. Inside the box he finds only a drowned rat. Encyclopedia adjusts the box's antennas and the picture looks much better.

When Ravished Left Behind

A baby will cry when it hungers inner thighs
...an unexpected bonus. Seeking
to establish a more personal education
should be discontinued. Maverick
condoms are on sale when I say
that you are handsome. Sometimes,
when the neighbors won't
be pretty. In Rio she executed
the fact that she was neglected
as a child. He didn't like [____]
to wear a butt plug for
eight hours before doing such
a thing in broad daylight?

The heightened sensitivity of maligned
fears along the rapport suggested he was
least. Had this dance going asunder.
Want to walk down the street for its mother's
milk. I heard a porn star say that the
need asked for her number. She had
a piercing—they would do such a thing—
including the use of power tools
and so on. When oil is struck
a geyser of the slick truths
are going at it (I touch myself).
Traditionalists will argue that sex-
foul-substance spurts high into the air.

Can you believe that she was, to say
politely, an anal scene? Her angst stems

from the eight inches: such as chainsaws,
in our region. The custody battle
for you, for a spa, exists in two theaters.
Our obligations, as children, all
had to endure six to veritable,
you know, down there, a blindness.
I hope I'm not being too forward
down at the drug store four
going for a dollar.
We're supposed to get forgotten
in these wretched days of iniquity.

I clip a coupon
and get some coffee?
Chastity and virtue are large-gauge
drills, a tour de force of debauchery.

Agency of Expense

in actuality we expect him to buy her
something of a present—*after all, she's*
and there was a broken conversation lying
at the bottom of a double barrel—*the mother of his children*
if only they sold cleverness as condominiums
the gift wrap would have a chance—*there's no time-and-a-half*
to impress their real estate agent and menopause planner
with missing teeth—*in their labor, in their union*

Fashionable Victim

The gentle one is slick-
sickened with staunch dents
and dings decorating
their exterior.

Tommy Hilfiger tried to launch
a dying nun into space as
part of an ad campaign.
Humanity as a whole

changed the channel.

He who waits should be
well-advised to watch
(but he won't, the dim bulb).
One eye watches the other.

Saintly broken bits smolder
on reentry, burnt prayers
merely smoke signals, as fashion's
martyr repossesses the Earth.

Calcified

women have
their temperature
orange lies
right fight
just smile
direct whimper
same temperature

sold God
partial medicine
slow suffer
wrong punishment
most suffocate
down sound
pray the

bone

invasive luxury
now revolve
harsh sever
half murder
sinew beast
tongue grist
breast point

sold her
whole neck
tomb drum
lion love
snack option
snake ink
suffocate hug

cage

Love Poem #1968

1

I will profane you excepting molest…

2

For the sake of everyone involved I had to throw the milk out.

3

a) MMM — by my troth! That be some fine booty…
b) "Oh! How dare you!"

4

a) "If you force me to remove my bra [at gunpoint] I will do so with pride."
b) If that's going to be her attitude I will feel guilty and look away.
c) Just pull the trigger already!

5

a) She's got "The Look" and the heart of a mad dog. Did she keep the heart? Ingest it? Does it beat within her breast? If so, that's a strange place for a heart (I guess that's why we men are heartless, eh?).
b) Blue, ice blue, sky blue, pastel blue…I envy them all.

6

Cemeteries of the temporary centuries…

7

Her flavor should not be known to mortals.

8

How can you sleep?

9

At work I worry about home; at home I worry about work.

10

Don't bother judging me.

11

The one thing you learn in life is that there's nothing you can do but rip your own child's throat out with your teeth if you want to get ahead.

12

a) She reveled in the carnage. The broken nose was, above all else (pain and humiliation included), a badge of honor. The shotgun in her hands was an Olympic torch (light on the "limp" but heavy on the big "O"). The screams cheered her on. Has she gone insane or is it just me?
b) She has been with child. *No! Pregnant*, curse your sick mind! I will not contemplate any other interpretation, nor shall I tolerate it in others. Refer to #11 above, although that was a self-reference and does not reflect on her or her child-rearing in any way, although I do find myself reflecting on her rear quite often.

13

Recipe for a strung-out mind: well-burned grits (made with milk, not water, and not that milk I had to throw out either, damn it all [don't try to get smart on me now — readers are supposed to be "gentle," remember?] — but hey, no harm no foul, as they say, so let us move on), two tablespoons margarine, two peanut butter cups. Stir while hot…stir crazy when consumed.

14

a) With a handful of hair he held her against the mirror. Sure, differing shades of red were decorating her face by that point, but I was feeling more violent than he regardless.

b) However helpless she was under the circumstances I was even less capable of rendering him lifeless.
c) To circumvent the circumstance was impossible, that was my stance so I could only vent.

15

[at which point one must admit that I look like a mushroom in my photographs]

16

I'd seen her a total of four times, growing more impressed with each successive encounter, before realizing that I had been *meeting the same person*. She can be tricky like that.

17

No eclipse on record — irrespective of its mystical nature, sublimity, or fear-inducing power — could surpass her majesty, usurp the place of the portents just concealed by her pupils. One shared trait between them is the transfixing nature of the illumination born of their darkness…and yes, looking directly into her radiance can induce blindness (even through a telescope all the way down here 3,000 miles below her).

18

a) I watch them sitting there clapping blandly and think, "Yep…if I had a gun leveled at their heads they'd be a hell of a lot more enthusiastic."
b) "They might even remove their undergarments, appreciatively no less." It goes without saying that I'd feel guilty as all get-out under those circumstances.

19

This has nothing to do with Pennsylvania.

20

In the name of the repressed geriatric proletariat masses I refuse to turn down the music.

21

a) What the hell, her sister ain't that bad either…
b) Oh, so they get freaky like that?! I, for one, refuse to believe libelous lies and slanderous slop (although the thought will, in fact, keep me "up" late at night).
c) Let's move to Utah!

22

a) Last I heard she killed him dead.
b) Elvis dropped in.
c) Every girl and boy need a little joy.

23

I'm looking to fail.

24

a) The jury is dead.
b) "Life" is an anagram. File. Lief. Ifle.

25

I feel so cool (you only have to tell me once, thank you).

26

female
holding
 and important position

in religious
or
o
ther
female
parent,
especially of
addres
s
to
anno
unce again or anew; to
devise,
make,
or construct,
as
off
spring
;
to bring
to
fabricate.
Mo
ther
me

27

Frustrations, inanities, and the need to relieve my bladder: I submit that there is a correlation.

28

a) If by "liking it rough" you mean homicide then yes — a thousand times yes — she likes it rough.

b) I never did resist.

29

a) Some of us are ashamed of our bodies.

b) Feathers are an extension of the skin; however naked a bird is it remains obscured by its skin, unlike humans.

c) Maybe birds of a feather will stand naked together.

30

Being “An Innocent Man” is BJ’s area of expertise; leave me to my specialties, which can be mined in the province of inexplicable dementia (emphasis on the “demon”).

31

If ageless beauty were a burden her back would be broken.

32

She’s made bedroom pugilism the celebrated pastime it is today.

33

a) I’ve never met anybody with prehensile breasts.

b) Let’s make an atom bomb. What’s that you say? Please allow me to demonstrate (no need to comment on that again).

34

I’d better just slap myself, wake up, and get on with my life.

Adult Money-Making Pussy Cam Increases Your Debt While You Sleep

I n c r e a s i n g S e x u a l P o t e n c y Your Friends Are Online and Want 4 Free Minors g86113 because they FOUND IT! Very Mature Adult Silvia Saint Flicks - No (200540) Alicia Webb can you copy?

Yipeee!! Interactive Cams, Videos & Pics of snot & dominga stilts will improve profitability: How to Get Out of Debt with REAL Viagra! So claim money you never knew you fathered 0004830458 And say: I chose life?

Burn your own Valentine's Roses - $29.99 a dozen, $54.99 for two!

Innocent Sister's BOY is only 15 and MAKES $71,000 IN 5 WEEKS - Here's How: Cash in on the 3 GUYS who MAKE HER MOAN ALL NIGHT with VIAGRA! ONLINE YOUNG TEEN DOES Dropping Interest Rates when they're Low, no shit 3754

Would you like to lose weight while you sleep, you Adult - See More Of Heather by Working at Home & Making More Hot XXX! Only Jeremiah Madelline is Over 21 and Needs More CASH FLOW 19776

Experience Success in MY CHAT ROOM and secret Online Knowlege Cam…

Make lenders breaks walls with your celeb pics 6474 Attention all Gamblers, GUARANTEED Winnings you fuckers! FoundMoney Drawing Winner Your brain is redundant Confirmation Number 1qEpmHjXG it only gets better?

How's your pension? Don't be "enron-ed" Easily_Attract_Women: your pension versus your PENISion! Attract The Opposite Sex by Making 45% on your money, be Fully Screwed Secure Schoolgirls - Flashers deduction (stripped mothers still smell) 4158

The Unhuman Perversions!!!!!!!!!!

DVD with CD RW? Not on your life - get FREE Pics of fat Mortgage Rates! 8====> Accept Credit Cards with your massive cock, SKYROCKET Your BUSINESS [sike] 20696 GailGBartels3874 Your attn: Positive notification, top priority.

Heat it up your lovetime life today when We pay you up to $1,000.00 a month to Reduce Debt For FREE! Feel Young HOT, YOUNG AND NASTY Opportunities of the Millennium [sike-a-boo-boo]...Eerie Jennifer Rowe?

GOV GRANTS, NEVER REPAY....FREE book: Make a living with demonology!

Cash in on the Dropping Interest Rates XLQCA...Would You Like To Travel And Vacation For FREE...FREE/INSTANT ONLINE MORTGAGE FINANCERS WHO LOVE ANIMALS!

Wet Soaked Phone Sweeties say: Don't get left stranded without a pussy PARTY ALL NIGHT! GO OVER VIAGRA FALLS ONLINE if you Want more money [TRY WORK] Congratulations, You Won $30 Today! And I'm a jerk...

L@@K Fossil: Free 24 hr Delivery + Double Miles for Valentines Freaky Farm Sluts ayX/ALMl/wA!!

An Elliptical Love

Darkness illumination…or
the…out loud wicked…you
drunken-loved me…and the throbbing
of your heart…added…a
deafening sort…your ears were not
big enough…to catch the sound
of…wicked loud outings…or
the illuminating darkness…
about…I don't know how
you could drink…could you
spare some ridiculously used
thrombosis…everybody knows it:
I loved you the roundabout way
…borrowing ten dollars today…
to stretch your heart with the
…interest, fucker.

Heathens Gathered at the Feast

Eccentric rises tidal and
unfulfilled, heavens
to Betsy be denied.

Sloppily he raises
a toast, a quiver,
an inexorable faint.

The general consensus
and corporal decision
is that drooling on the floor

is uncomely.

Fist served on sterling
silver-mane apes aroused
by the flight of the squeamish

thesaurus is declared solicitously
tasteless. Nobody cares.
The eccentric continues to drool.

The sergeant of primeval
orthodontia and footwear decides
to modify etiquette for

the purpose of cohabitation.

BLOODCLOT

Cruel Low
Offensive
Consum
mashun
Blonde Dagga'
Foucauldian
Dismis
sez
Conspicuouz
Lazy Objectifiez Offense
Driftz

Brutal Lunch
Cigar
Lion
Losez
O'erwrought
Outlook
Brill
iant
Stiflin'

Brill
iant Stiflin'
Optimal
Wasted Lazy
Obsc
ene
O'erwrought
Outlook Caushunary

Wasted
Lazy O'er
reachez
Ons
la
ught
Deadly Laughz Outcome
Offense DelicaC
C@alyst
Courageouz Leopard
Orderz Turnz
Omniscient Loud
Organ
Omnipo10t Dam
ned
O'er
reachez
Blonde
Dagga' Foucauldian Laughta'
TasT O'er
reachez Ons
la
ught

Deadly Laughz
Outcome Offense Omniscient
Omnivorouz
Delic8
C@
Little Lazy O'er
reachez Blonde
Losez

O'erwrought CrEpz
Language
Turkey

Deadly CrEpz
Observez Meta-morphz
Bizar
re
Lo'a'
Opshun
Optimal
Op
posez Omniscient
Loud
Organ Omnipo10t
Temptashun
Stiflin'
Oscill
8z
Omni
present
Dip
TasT-Biological
Lovely
Lookz
Outcome T
exture
Lazy
Deadly CrEpz
Language O'ersize 2rture
Blue

There Must've Been a Sale on Uncles

One year my father took me out
to the woodshed and breathed me.
Twelve months later he sterilized
his nipple with a cornish hen. Our dog,
a mixed German Siamese, licked
at my pants while my mother decided that
she was old enough to take care
of herself. I didn't even get it
and ended up marrying somebody
that didn't make sense.

She's really very upset about it. A little
teenager said, *Oh sugar!* the way
Mussolini might have ordered a cocktail.
Reminds me of how I used to spit
on the floor if a girl wiggled her
scalp at me. In my family we just don't
abide rudeness (or token aneurisms).

Beyond the Islands

My bitter worship
manipulates these rusting cars,
could pound above an

ugly blue girl…stop

incubating a sea man
you rip a sweet diamond
symphony whore ship

Insight Erasure

French classes broke out during an afternoon eruption
of eucalyptus oil anonymously identified as “lazy.”
Yes, I do think that’s bizarre, in an improved,
healthy kind of way.

Caustic substances scolded Scotland
Yard baffled in bereavement, cemented in
what was meant once, twice; resembling a complimentary
sample which was “involved”—so to speak—with cowardice
and the coward’s ice and, really, why

should a tour guide have pictures of prostitutes
on the cover? I thought it was odd
when the service was awful, perhaps a bad day aghast.

No efficiency.

A French toll of 305 was reported in East Delhi
today, Ted Koppel said while finally self-flagellating
and declaring that “we don’t accept cash!”

Let him on, the train has already burned.
Prostitutes cuddled the unwanted lovechildren
born of the complimentary sample and the cowardice,
oozing caustic lessons

from lesions of imperialistic *grandeur*
(those French classes finally paid off).

Half-Assing It

I've screamed to exotic locales, fellated
computer games, gone model train Fancying
...that stuff costs money.
Too: book collecting, skydiving, travel to pay
+ don't want to see a webzine (or for a word at least
slap yourself). The past twenty-five years or informal
basis, want to be ME—What the past twenty-five
years of informal bias became is ME—What
the demands of business plans are snorting:
solicit work and go down. If someone doesn't
want to be delivered, or start a gun
then pay 3-5 cents a word and meet me over
at The Very Least. The market HAS made itself
very clear over the demands, of course...what happened?

I've yet to pay that much, because the chances
I'll put my money in my mouth is the market,
which HAS spoken, and if someone doesn't want
to pay that matter, to anyone's head to see a publisher
go out and secretly despise their closet life. I've
seen plenty go out of the womb to start a webzine
(or for that matter, to be delivered, or I). Nobody sits around
waiting for a hobby, great, let it be taken seriously,
they don't want to anyone's head to make them sign
contracts and promise money they were half-assing
it to be delivered, I I I I I, want to be a publisher.
Start a webzine for content providers.
I will, if it's a free parachute.
WHY WON'T YOU LISTEN TO exotic locales,
computer games, model train fancying, book collecting,

skydiving, travel to anyone's head to make them. They
need to see a little hollow. I wouldn't complain if someone
doesn't want to see anyone's head pay that much. The demands
I I I I start a little hollow. I wouldn't complain if I wouldn't
complain. Someone doesn't want to be ME. The market HAS
spoken and short story markets run on the demands of very
clear demands. Good work goes down. If they don't
pay + miracle happens = profitable success for a hobby.
This is based in part on a free parachute.

Part A: Free Parachute
Or, WHY WON'T YOU LISTEN TO Anyone's Head

what you're doing + miracle happens = profitable success or itself HAS made itself very deserving + as nobody is a hobby I is based in part on a hobby but hobbies cost money to ME - what you're doing + do it + don't pay that much - they were half-assing it x overpaid x they knew they didn't have ad hoc complaints about ME + poverty ring a gun + nobody put a gun to pay anything ME=what they deserve sign contracts and novels before anybody bought one...the market will bear exotic locales fancying they were half-assing it + don't want to + do it + such business because it be delivered, or I I I ME know what you're doing + don't want nobody x sitting around = nonprofit, or what they don't pay + miracle - everybody loves me = I am an informal biASS

Now at Your Command

leak	me	damp
power	still	tenuous
dull	effect	split
now	crunch	hell
pay	scrape	collapse
run	road	long
men	mine	strain
try	lance	enjoy
egg	chisel	leak
pray	evolve	suffer

Planned Cityhood

depopulating sand-worn hues
(in need of fabric softener) I
found contention's complete
skeleton among the blistered walls.
with lonesome studs of hegemony waiting
in the wings for unsuspecting contractors
to pass carelessly through their
ruins only to find themselves
gang-violated, bearing a litter of splinters
I harden my heart and seek to address
your mesoblasted blocks, building
a bridge to your immature state.
Should I doctor your designs?
In so doing I may once again set
to this business of rekindling death
among this pockmarked populace
—afflicted with running colors—
and chuckle faintly to myself
watching red stumble on a collarbone,
squeal when purple brains itself on a jaw
and light the structure afire
with pernicious embitterment
at another contractor's haste.

Where You Can Get Screwed

the creative way to be ignorant
is to be a corporate reporter: it would
benefit the advertisements if we
worked very slowly with preheated styles

embroiled outside of a mortgage
company's coming over for help. and to
borrow half a cup of effect (that might be
some adjustable misunderstanding)

An Experiment Gone Awry

Ironically enough Joe Mormon dienged to call me no whore now! So facile, what was the contraversy in time release medicines (undiscovered). There was some sort of this type—indiginous despair—of dastardly gel hub-bub. "Mum's wasn't it? The claim is that no matter how vigorous an effort is made I prefer not to leave Sandra out of…that's not really a Mormon." Mum's the hub-bub, her contraversy conserved a spotlight, no matter how dim, facilities were whored. Joe Mormon mouthed despair regarding the Buddist monastary and discovered (in time) it was all about…? Let's claim this: slack morals. "Don't you leave the word," he released to me. "Navy S.E.A.L.'s in the zoo, word." [poor attempt at slang; attempt at murder on the rise] Terrible about Sandra, gelatinified in the tub. Let's eat some of that with a spoon, shall we? Curiously one will not find no speak of fornicators and their hill there, where it was, I swear to you! I swear to you at sixty miles per hour, across the MPAA's cencorious superhighway of ill intent. Noting it's condition the government ordered intent hospitalized. Time release medicine failed to restore vigorous hell(th). Nevermind that dental hygiene—indiginous spotlight—is at the bottom of my list, if you must know. Up on the boy Sandra will be benifitial symptoms, my friend.

Proxy War

We can survive a Parliament:
that country which our country owns.
Our country owns that country; the person
deputed to act for another has been constructed
whose goal is to overthrow our government.
I always wash my display of avarice!
There have been three wars involving
the disclosed outrage (after another).
Please delineate the difference,
Ghandi in the white!
Islamabad has no ethnic
minorities disenfranchised. Systematic
rape and torture training camps
which are used to train insurgents are
devices in the no-man's land
between Pakistan and India. She considered
that perhaps [who] would use nuclear
weaponry on neighboring countries.
A veritable Berlin Wall was jaded.
The agency of a person who acts as a substitute
is treacherous. He did not care for curry;
tradition was not the best way to go.
The enemy is harboring a guerilla employed
by the occupying forces to keep the number
of warheads in its nuclear arsenal (accountant).
It was just one the two nations within the hands
when I come home. What a disgusting
last fifty years. The attack on the
nuclear attack, yes, I do enjoy the scars,
but our enemies would be

destroyed by the last straw. Fight, fight,
if you will, between the suicide bombers
and the heads of state; a nuclear war.
The minefields form a principal;
authority to act for another; your country
does not own his palate of minefields.

And the Sickness Issues Forth

an elaborate garden incubates truth
I cook iron moons and yet after
cooly parting your purple dress—
like clubbing a life, an only need—sleep
is produced like a near trip...they have
mostly let all sagging go as none
so we embrace delirious summer need
a raw repulsive shadow goddess
this luscious finger in blue;
dreamlike chant fluff cavorts with
DIAMOND SAUSAGES
music must tell of rose rust
and how one said "use sweet
mad woman-girls as beds"
or perhaps sulking rotisserie grills
of dry-skinned condemnation flaking one sin
at a time for all eternity

Waste Can

Can you broaden your back in homage
to the clouds of truth damning the skies:
a therapeusis written in the confines
of a ghetto will inseminate what
we refer to as a “licorice totem pole”.

Can you explain with an unbaptized
tongue how Catholicism was spread
to Eurasia by Native Americans: I
challenge you to get a job drinking
honey mustard test products.

Can you explain how the Californian stole
my floppy, my monitor, my hairdo
with a deadbeat doctor: it’s too much
having the agents of fertility running
the machines of destitution.

PC Anatomy

The nose should be digestion. The lips should be deception. The eyes: a menagerie of iridescent beetles scrabbling from one carcass to the next. Skin should, generally, be yellowish in tone twenty-five percent of the time, reddish in tone seventy percent of the time.

It is sixty-three percent certain that the personality is radish and the desires a menagerie-a-trois of entomological plight. The corpus of a life's work should be radiant—but we all know better. The hopes should be corporeal while the intent remains heavenly thirteen percent of the time.

The general should be a corporal if his skin is bright and clear (which is to say, ladylike). He knows we all hope to remain thirteen-year-olds. That alone is a reason for giving him a demotion. We'll see if he's as thick-skinned as they imply with their decorations. His men should move at his command, a swarm with but one hive mind.

Ladies in the armed forces should be hard, rough, like cheese graters. They should work in demolition teams no greater than twenty-seven percent of the corps. Otherwise, we all know the hopes of the corporal. Undigested intent should kill a seventy-five-year-old. Decorum demands that personality should be mangy.

A Conversation from Below

that night you came across a used anal probe and drank lemonade I sang
to you, meaningless notes

wasted paper breath

you always were the one who knew how to tune
out every organ, slut-chuckles quivering

through your flesh

and your typewriter touch sent the mysterious night sirens
wailing, which always inspires feelings of helplessness

spiraling through me

Cataratchet

the spectacle of dilettante revelation
is trifocal, a monocle
a pinochle-dealt brandy monochrome
of inane hesitation, dire
churning in the loins for hairless nights
of innocent reverie, a spectator's
voyeurdrenalyne rush hour
moistening that thrice-sullied
dangling glass, the cards you've been dealt
forming the epicenter of inebriation
and insane fire clouds
burning within your bladder
with revered surges of angst
straining to break free, as eyes squint
oh! the shame of losing a contact
a friend or a reality
awash with the elucidating
complexity of being wrong

Nature vs. Nurture, Final Round

for two months he tried to get by
just eating Ding-Dongs and Ho-Hos
it didn't work; he ended
up in the hospital emergency
room and some asshole intern gave
him a Twinkie, well boy-howdy I'll
tell you him flipped a right trick
upside a little somethin'-somethin'

didn't make sense much he was born
ramblin' (you know what I mean)
heads: fare thee well, he's bound
to die on the train between ontology
and the cardiac ward painted sugar-
white to aid in getting the sickly
to sleep or so I've heard tell
and maybe friends think it's all a
stranger's crapshoot on God's golden
shores (porcelain fixtures and linoleum
tiles, people, etc...you KNOW what I mean)

there's been a driver down one time
too many and the factory-formed
pastries just don't cut it no
more so the doctor recommended a healthy
dose of insulin but our boy was hard
of hearing and swored the dude was
talking about that newfangled fiber
glass spun out like cotton candy;
more sweets, from the insides of the walls no less

Gene Splicing

Young studs marched up and down the sperm bank and made an unlicinsed withdrawal. With ankles shall we to like an arson facilited by the use of [_]? Eggs may be one heavy scene…they are known to be so. Orgies fertilized it to her. (Let's be any number of ways.)

Like matador's entrails strung between a loathesome act and a quarrelsome intermission: every touch denied complicity.
"So yeah, like, her titties were a sign of the systemic insemination in animals by plastics. Along all the Nile there has been an upswing in the gradual degeneragtion of the Roman Empire."

Can you dream me? Can you dream me now, dancing?
"Nudes will find a plethora of lovely photo ops."
Only your failure could be my shame.
"No, she wasn't. That's when she was strapped, that is, began to strip. You know."
—you suck, you suck—

"That's what marriages are for." Gotta hand it to the hopes of a lucid fur, a devil with ringing ears, a wakeless rest on the road of good intentions; I was like that, right? That must've been a sight for bad boys—in with the sheep and the oxen. Artificial, if you will, fell overboard. What do I mean? I mean it fell out of the dictionary and died! "On the river?" Think about it, there's like a rubber mill what with colonialization and shit that would mean…?

"Yeah man…" I now declare Artificial Memorial Day.
The humilation was more than public, it was personal.
"Far from being born, it stops without, killing it." The convent was huge man, I mean some mama-jamas. The nipples on them burned to the

ground. Interacial man, know, uh, some tough shit.
I sold more than you...
A robber broke into the headboard! "On the boat, that's how we found him. Cursed is he who layeth the law in most provinces. Polygamy is against the main thoroughfare/monster. YANG attracting a virgin's eye and much, much more! In recent years the condoms...now...hey, you crocodiles there?"

The way you've humiliated me in front of everyone.
Inside, her moonlight had never been so serious. I felt an unplussed gratitude swarm-swelling in my left palm and let it communicate with her face directly.

People want a pricey product, they want to feel like it's out of reach. It needs to be elitist, elite listed, elite black list, the elevation of blacks is low on the list. Jack up the price.

He'll be deformed, don't you know that? The Good Book says to slay those who would mingle. Isn't that what parties are for? Don't the politics of marriage dictate that a pound of flesh is worth a comprimise, and vice versa?

I'll get there late and leave early, and no: don't ask me to look at art damn you!

(it really is all about me, isn't it?)

Chicago Jarman

I aim to get it crunk with
bent tears and a bottle of boobs

She did it her way because she thought
I was being a little helpful

or something

You could probably have more...
You could find a place for it...

It's a crunchy nature fixation
we dare to liquify without smoke

it never was a very good one

Spilling the Battle

alabaster sin coated crumbling
chrome plating, a residual
resident's duel in the lunch room
chalky white smears of hideous
shaming one and all, swearing

"If only I could deep throat
a goldfish, a vine (a noose or
nourishment?) and purchase seven
extra battles of polish for
the discontinued sterling
and those somewhat despicable
plates!" [effeminate applause followed

by teeth being knocked out]
go chew on that gramps
the pimply gumline denotes
five dollar favors and sewage
flavored saviors four for ten
dollars, get your rebate

now only seventeen dollars
wallboards should be made
to crumble and leave us
with no room

to hate, to hang
posters or photographs of ourselves
repulsed by the scent of our
disinterest

Cable TB

stricken by purple-lipped erectile
pining I delighted in the mirage
allowing another step to be taken
to vote on the floor of localized
tourism pledging its allegiance
to national prime-time spots

schisms erupted by auto-erotic strangulation
threatened to upgrade to category four
through false addition, the methodology
of addiction—to a smiling face
be damned through string bean teeth
(eternity means nothing when you're shucking corn)

add gravy! the ensemble doesn't work
without lumpy fat and flour
to vivisect at will/to call
home where the fart is (you brute)
and I can feel the distinct sting
of humiliation waiting in the wings

consumption lodges another lump of lung
in the feeding tube, allowing no room
for pork to cruise through flesh channels
to be deranged in one final act
with no lines, no actors, only a colorful
rage, delightful and weeping having taken
its last step

PC OD

The way he can become a deformity without hesitation. The way he is one moment the chameleon verb, the lynx noun, the stingray indefinite article. The way he was never meant to be.

He didn't mean to be hesitation without deformity. The desire was to be bounding through wet forests, careening around lush coral graveyards, the silent voyeur digesting insects. He simply lacked the words.

In sex deformity is his "verb": lipos**ting, breast aug***ting, nip and t**king, and for the finish collagen inj**ting. It's a simple lack of graveyards that necessitates honeymoon suites.

Neil Armstrong discovered that the Moon is made of honey, not cheese as was formerly postulated. What a sweet, horrible death he had—in every position, as he sank to the Moon's core. His corpse drifted on indefinite tides, silent, wishing he had hesitated before plunging into that celestial graveyard.

Invention, the Bad Son

To
concoct;
to
contrive

and
produce; to portray or
re
present;
to anno
unce again
or re
present; to
renew

the
originator
of addres
s to
fram
e
by
the
production
of;
to concoct; to
fabricate. Mo
ther
me
mo

ther
fuck
mo
ther
hell mo
ther

love
smo
ther
ing
mo
ther
ing
smo
ther

smo
ther
hell reproduce: to
elderly
females; an abes
s
or
re
present; to portray
o
ther
female
holding

and important position

in religious
or
o
ther
female
parent,
especially of
addres
s
to
anno
unce again or anew; to
devise,
make,
or construct,
as
off
spring
;
to bring
to
fabricate.
Mo
ther
me
mo
ther
fuck
mo
ther
hell
mo

ther

love

smo
ther
ing
mo
ther
ing smo
ther

smo
ther
hell
reproduce:
to anno
unce again or re
present;
to
generate, as
the
memory
or
o
ther

female parent, especially of
something
that did not

exist

before;
to
contrive
and produce; to contrive

and produce;
to
fabricate.
Mo
ther
me
mo
ther
fuck
mo
ther
hell
mo
ther

love
smo
ther
ing
mo
ther
ing smo
ther

smo
ther
hell

reproduce:
to
fabricate. Mo
ther
me mo
ther
fuck
mo
ther
hell
mo
ther

love

smo
ther
ing mo
ther
ing smo
ther

smo
ther
hell
reproduce:
to anno
unce
again or construct,
as
off
spring

; to
renew

the
imagination; to
excogitate;
to fram
e by
the
memory or
semi-religious
institutions; i
nvent: to fabricate. Mo
ther
me
mo
ther
fuck
mo
ther
hell
mo
ther

love

smo
ther
ing mo
ther
ing
smo

ther
smo
ther
hell reproduce:
to
anno
unce again
or
imagination.
Mo
ther
:
a fam
iliar
term
of
the production of;
to anno
unce again or
re
present;
to
fabricate.
the hu
man
race;
a
female parent,
especially
of something

that

did
not

exist
before; to
bring
to contrive

and
produce;
to
fabricate.
Mo
ther
me
mo
ther
fuck
mo
ther
hell
mo
ther

love
smo
ther
ing
mo
ther
ing
smo

ther
smo
ther
hell
reproduce: to
concoct; to
anno
unce again
or
re
present; to
concoct; to
devise,
make,
or o
ther

female parent, especially of something
that
which
has
borne a
female
parent,
especially of addres
s to
bring to
elderly
females; an abes
s
or
anew;

to

the hu
man

race;
a
child;
that which has
produced
anything;
generatrix;
a fam
iliar
term
of
the
originator
of
something
the
memory
or semi-religious institutions; i
nvent: to renew

the
originator
of

the
hu
man

race;
: a
fam
iliar
term of
the
hu
man
race;
a child;
that did not

exist
before;
the
memory
or
re
the
imagination; to
excogitate;
to concoct

The Plague Factory

The toil never, ever
rusts completely under the gore-glaze
and the illness-lusting consumer
demand. Fetid flesh stench
rises lazily—

Serious membranes accompany the glandular tumefactions; furthermore,
cloudy swelling of the internal organs, and sometimes hematuria

—because the pus-filled skin sack is
no longer scandalous. Its pendulous folds
contain the tremors of celebrity.
Gristle grinding so sublime smothers
every scream unkind and otherwise:
the purpled escapdes of bacterium that should be
coveted by the cultured
inane realities of decay are
dripped to, spoonfed, slipped
on and slipped through…

carbuncles also develop, most frequently upon the inferior extremities.
Panophthalmitis, followed by total blindness, may occur within,

(fetishized hell granules lumber about mindlessly absorbing the
cream-like despair, green in their way, and yet unavoidable somehow,
strangely obscure to the naked empathy, and flameless under the
myopic attentions of the suicidal)

Plague does quietly.
Plague worries for our carcinogenic

world; plague flies! Plague quotes busily,
clinically, she pursues.
Plague longs for support from
her pronouncement, retreats from her
explanation, gets used to her anachronism:
the sputa of specific bacilli.

possibly rupturing externally. The affected organs, and erysiplelas, etcetera! The amoral particular pathos

The bacillius of pneumonic cases,
in the pus from her arm, wants gifts
from this large smelly mammal; man-plague
feels for our carcinogenic world.

becomes the skin, mucus and serious membranes, in order to accompany the pathos, containing the swollen glands which are superficial. They produce the abstinence.

Punctiform hemorrages of technology are
said frequently to be favored
by vermin, especially rats.
This is a bad time for love.
The onset is usually sudden.

Permissive Decadence

A noxious daughter understands endlessly (she would, the perverse brat). A spider ogles comprehendingly (he is a naughty one, no?). Daughter's nudism (I should do so well): a deciding spider's disinterested comrade (better clean up the mess).

God changes the diaper on his aspect every second you are watching. Happy indeed is the writer who can recognize all his disguises. At one moment God is a zero, a smoky ejaculation, the next he's the cable-TV installer contriving aneurisms, doing unspeakable things on a hydrant, or the little girl (nudist go slap yourselves!), or perhaps the enchanting smoky contraction of a cataract-eye refusing to dilate.

The unitary sound splitting is offering us earaches at a pliable price; it is rare that barnacles climax for religion, but the religion offered soullessly by such a monstrously humid sound is not to be construed as danger, acts of terrorism, or antisocial values. It stinks under the arm for us. No strict delineation should be considered to be derived from games. It is the religion cut on the crackpot of the human privacy...defected, as this vast force acting upon itself. In this new mutilation we will not find the playmates of the backside so long sought after by philosophers and theologians. What we will find is a criticism of ourselves, a bit of eloquent hide-and-seek in which we realize that no competitions as such can be found. We would like to make the excitement. We deceive easily some crackhead in the mirror.

We never should understand the captivation of a scantily arbitrary redhead. Should we attempt to impale ourselves, no brilliant splash will reduce our mourning to rubble—for secluding a scientific (if irrational) objectivity—since we know that the yield truthfully lies in the performance, or thereabouts. Failure to perform without coarseness means pure cowardice, blasphemy, or bibliophilism, just as the sludge-toting nonperformance of singularly pretty petals means the antidote of nymphomania is kindhearted cannibalism. Comprising, calling endlessly—"love of hand"—and detaching for all that you hold valuable should be acts of organization, not of nerd.

The cosmic aphorism is offering us the pathetic cacophony for religion, but the religion offered by such a generous aphorism is not at least one imagination of reassurances or bashful values. It postpones for us no strict delineation of domains or geniuses. It is one religion objectified on the highway of human deformity energized, as a masculine force acting upon itself. Oh my! In this new earlobe we will not find the nullifications of the element so long sought after by philosophers and theologians. What we will find is the slumber of human nature, a bit of cybernetic self-discovery in which we realize that no circuitries as such can be found. We make the authenticity. We deprecate the probability.

Only quite contemporary people outside of the resonances know how to speak acceptance with demeanor. They make photogenic powers of animalism, music, and the kings, but their biased jewel is willowy, a flat altar in the automaton, and an optimistically careful parasitic fiction which far surpasses emperors of snowy paranoias, essential hills or probabilities, female furies, and mysterious circuses, escapisms, or conversations, and even rotted pathological psychologies. No one is plumper than the patient of this epoch, for he is the very arrogant chimney sweeper.

Only arbitrary people riding the performances know how to pester exception with paranoia. They make ambitious principles of deference, scummy ponds, or the spiders, but their dark glass is mossy, a flat coat in the bell, and a hopeful exuberant and macho pretension which far surpasses cities of silvery circuses, phony expressions and odds, tasty ineptitudes, and delicate times, beetles, and breakouts, or even slender, deathly elephants. No one is more able than that guitar player of Bodice, for he is a very bashful gardener.

An ordinary mail man who lived in Vancouver lived in constant fear of frightened desolation. He decided to study Freudian theology. In the course of his studies, he met John Kennedy, at that time very noble, who cured the problem with his aristocratic water. "Golden," he called it. Our little ordinary mail man (now strong and Christian) started a rat farm instead and lived happily, if realistically, ever after.

A falling confession clouds criminally; the fox who offends placidly. Confession's employment, an extricating fox's sinister centralizer.

We understand at least one gainful degradation of cheery exposure. We show something to no one, which is to say, a luxurious euphemism for stinking up your underused imagination, since we know that the outlook lies in the performance. Failure to perform means neurotic despair or bananas, just as the nonperformance of ageless paradigms means the alcohol of wine. Oppressing hopefully, slavering enticingly, we imitate the über class rebellion against Pearl Jam, and find it empowering. Janice Joplin's cold crotch should be acts of "sugar," not of "competition." Now put that in your pipe and smoke it!

We never understand a shout of catastrophic breadth. We give things to no outlandish era for deciding the current political environment, since we know that the cowboy lies in the performance. Failure to perform means brainwashing or consecration, just as the nonperformance of emotional philosophers means the relationship of our playmate is sardonic. Supposing practically, needing placidly, we engage in rebellion against risk, and it is disaffecting for your personality to sleep on the television, not in the pity.

As my omniscient friend Mr. Diaz once timidly said to Ms. Moore, "They pretend it's easy to be strange, to be buzzed, but I know better. I say it. Perhaps of all famous feelings, I alone coerce. I know about convexity. Oh, yes, I know all about convexity! I know about his sentences and his religions. It is because of his domains that he is to be an orthodox ambition. Out of his powers has arisen a nirvana, not a Pearl Jam. I recover this nonconformist breath for him. I call it 'flambé.' I unscrambled up the spring when I was a jolly valet. Convexity, he is a want needing bureaucratic decency to be loved. He is something fatalities need from constancies."

Hey, it got Ms. Moore into the sack…it's good enough for me. More synergy to you, profound Mr. Diaz.

1) a proud answer possesses assiduously
2) a spider personalizes taming
3) answer's note,
4) a pestering spider's
5) argumentative log

The dying masses' paradoxical obsessions often point out the comfort the dying masses provide for the celebrated, the awe-inspiring, and the human. This is fine for them. But the biological friend must not dawdle in the decade zone! If one yearns to require things from the tooth of the Divine, one must not fail to examine the solidity, must certainly understand a whore, must come to observe fewer chestnuts, and hurt unto optimistic wrongs! One must detonate cordially the rewards of the evenings, the religions of damned notes! How comely, how prudently counteracting to think of the dying masses as a backbiting old man, as a rich doctor who requires that we accept simple deadly yachts, where the charismatic witch stirs too few nubile hawks with denigrated flakes of oft-mocked offshoots.

Such pathetic employment will debase a mephistophelean cab driver.

Beware of the certifications ahead! Already those existences are condensing, they pollute within in some specific elegance of armpits; it is a prevailing downer. Keep your mind on many/fewer perfectible loves, or the constructs developed by edible laughter in the anxious world! Face opposites under the exemplary ideas! Beware of the coming certifications!

The quivering decision mourns noiselessly. A bear loves slewing. Decision's mutilation, an acquitting bear's nude stalk.

"If Paul (insert surname here) were a mathematical underachieving ruler, then Bill Clinton would be a medieval outsmarting young woman," as the old saying goes.

Only quite callous people on top of the domains know how to vanquish forever queens with candor. They force green pleasures to flow, assurance, down the necks, but their cheery beverage is mossy, a quivering exaltation in the underwear, or an emotional kind of celestial nose which far surpasses fluffs of notorious authorizations, sensual denials or optimums, bitten eagles, and wild clichés, brinks, and demons, and even mathematical, emotional yields. No one is more precious than a close friend of deception, for s/he is more than one very anarchistic expert.

The charismatic psychic is bound to be turned by the combination, since he has precooked to avoid dissatisfying in cosmic performances or cancers of the irreplaceable reassurances I develop. He hugs perceiving to regard them as something extroverted, and, to use an analogy, drifted far from a father…he jumped a bittersweet lovely scandal without burning his feet. I trot out all the abortions that a cowboy contacting light, a formless rhythm etc., finds black, the abortions that the government produces without solving anything. I verbalize to those screamed abortions: you are quite correct, vitalize and demand at least one touchless blur!

He clouds backsides proudly; it is mathematical in nature. The one blinks and delineation ordinarily depreciates (now about performances, or, more truthfully, how privacy…defected, of confession's coarseness, with the disaffecting ahead!). Shout the least in such conversations, and debase your breath with a charismatic answer after. An omniscient rich cowboy is a cliché, an aristocratic fart is spring-like in its authenticity. That means abortions: slender, whore, abortions achieving rhythm to the coming of a gardener. He requires masses of cannibalism.

Prevails
with pupils,
cannibalism possesses
with addictions, cannibalism calms ordinarily
cannibalism slaves for the face
cannibalism lives for the outrageous organic slime…
Cannibalism hopes for intelligence

with pathways, cannibalism wants
cannibalism
begs for the right wing…
Cannibalism feels for
an admirable chastity that
she overshoots
cannibalism
lives for an attraction.
She looks to a single princess,
she gets used to her horror,
she looks to the altruism,
she shows it all to an easygoing egotism…
She throws something to a calculation.

Cannibalism needs
cannibalism runs,
cannibalism begs for a kind of aberration,
cannibalism yearns with ease she persuades brutally
cannibalism explains things to a leadership vacuum, takes to your hidden creativity, throws it to the Beach Boys, gives to a computer chip, takes things to my cold calculation,

with beatniks, cannibalism pampers gently
cannibalism suffers for
the brazen philosophy that she walks
she comes to the incoherent autumn,
she finds connections to a placid barren femininity:
she makes pathways to a shattered grin.
She goes to a personality…

Cannibalism penetrates slowly

On Adolescents, Or A Crimson Society For Hopeless Deans Of These Silent Silent Silent Silent Shrieks

[when we shake hands you'll know it]

Silent silent silent silent silent silent silent silent silent silent silent silent silent silent silent silent silent friendly teens. These hopeful silly deans. These hopeful silly silly silly silly silly silly silly deans. If blades refuse to penetrate those received facts: you and the physical philosopher are the wrongs of countless biceps, perpetuated on the jungle. The jungle.

The clinical climax relaxes, and societies of berserk games!

One must take it as it has always mocked those ____ __ ________ you are anxious, or or if an overwrought plateau holds enough honesty to keep track of terrorism, then the expressions of that virgin…dare I say it…calming on boats of religion coalesced…on the penetration! So long sought after by the next (that virgin ______ing on the perpetual, the eager victim who can recognize all the adult ____.)

And so, the virgin said, "We only need to keep track of enhanced spiders!"

So ends my treatise on the Battle of the Bulge (or are you just happy to see me?).

How whimsically enticing to the dull cable-TV installer. One must not expect to regard them as something joyous and be sadly demolished to say it. We will not except a joyful passing romantic, because then 20th century alienation would be stinky. Geniuses that sanitize the religion are offended by the diamond, not memories of your own bit of a fatally revolving emergency. A pathological plateau is bound to performances. Seek not memories! I know a minister of reassurances or what might put it. Perhaps that straighten the daybreak etc., Finds enhanced, the wrongs of nymphs, or a minister of a property of New York fiends was pricing fear for endless deans These silent friendly teens The conspiracies, the eery loved one. If fiends refuse to keep track of exuberant exhalations!

How stoking, how normalizing, how unexactly normalizing, how whimsically enticing to make pathways to injustices. What can recognize all her atlas-like dandruff? Not your coed dragon-duster. I trot out of uptown screens, dropping hope for the circumference to coin a captor, and must cleave to performances. Seek not "fail" to find "fail" is offering us the notorious fallacy!

An amoral seer: as an analogy, diminished from a variation! As injustices the 20th century alienation would be suckled, or what we confess with precooked pieces of cryptic hide-and-seek in resonances against laughter which we re-connect to thefts or merely an amoral seer (as something is bound to want chicks as acts of terrorism). The fresh profanity of the nubile world is cantankerous and depraved by New luck: we commence warily the extravagance of New luck: we confess with disgust the kind definitions with precooked pieces of deathly fingers, where that is truly important. We re-connect wrongs to think of this new glitter: we realize that we confess with flowed morsels of the perpetual. The Brady Bunch would be paranoid, a guy might put it. We realize that a fictitious crackpot ignores criminally, no entertaining snake's explorable shot.

In the comfort of this new luck we will find the white king must re-connect wrongs to injustices. What might start us.

Your own companion is baggage stuffed with chaste memories, sociably abjects, renewing religions for authoritarian slime. This adolescent is merely an odorous mountain. God changes her backwater! Every extraordinary money should regard them as something; it is enough honesty to find the nubile world wide web browser in a curfew, which must break out of cryptic hide-and-seek in which are anxious, or noxious values. It has always mocked the examined and the comfortable. Perhaps that exists. She loosens an ascent, since she has sewed to your mother's extroverted astrologies, often pointing out all tasty surfeits, I develop. She sews her aspect every second.

Blessed indeed is the highly desirable that sanitizes an alchemist who gives us a clenched pre-empting baby.

If the sign is humankind, their own zealous wife will find the ornamental force acting upon itself (oh! the debauchery!). In luxurious feelings and silence she sews her rotten ejaculation.

I empower to be belonged to, or clarified, whatever that might mean. It is highly desirable that a crimson society for authoritarian slime. This poem as such is a zipper, not memories against laughter which are quite correctly spinning tonight for injustices or to examine the overwrought principles. It to Mr. Munchkin once despairingly said, "To coin a horror and the circumference is to use an ecstatic extinguished sleeve, as with my friend Mr. Wilson, they pretend it's easy to inhale injustices."

What the clinical brown television endures, since she precooks a religion coalesced on top of thefts, regarding them as a curfew, we must break out all tasty surfeits, I have enough honesty to incubate.

What is the extravagance of vast hide-and-seek conferences in resonances and the alternative memories of nymphs, or something intoxicating, and sadly demolished to coin a great many possessions, untwine onto black domains?! One must not find salvation in the alternative memories of deathly fingers, where that something becomes joyous. Construction of vast hide-and-seek leagues in the clinical trials exposes the transcendent to life of enhanced spiders! How thankfully coexisting to be a gargoyle, she asks her backwater! Every second. Blessed indeed is the deistic, and to use an obligation. I develop.

She crawls perpetually to avoid acquitting organic injustices marinated in noxious values. It is homosexual to accept confessions as such a minister of reminded heavens.

The diamond, not the atmosphere climbing ambivalence apparatus, is comfortable. Perhaps that straightens the pleasures of humankind, retrofitted demonic companions of skill. At any time in these adolescent memories we realize that no psychologists are uniquely perverse. A cosmic stunt man searches all tasty surfeits, I alone declaim. A foul-mouthed fattening stranger. Their exotic oasis penalizes madly this cockroach, petrified by spinning. Oasis's song, this deafening cockroach's penitent river. The Kingdom of Pathos. At one moment God changes her atlas. We demand the property of thieves: those stolen astrologies, you, and reassurances. NASA keeps track of moldy civilizations, while a pan of pathos simmers. At one moment God changes her rotten ejaculation.

A lifetime of cryptic hide-and-seek with the injustice of geniuses cannot sanitize the alternative memories I develop. She loosens an extraordinary money, to say it. We will diversify the Divine, one must not fail to the kind definitions with flowed morsels of reminded heavens. An amoral seer, as the chasm zone!

The Brady Bunch would be unified, but phony resonances and therefore delicate extraordinary forces act upon them. In the deistic societies of flashes comfort that sanitizes quick, and construction is merely an extraordinary force acting upon clarifications of terrorism recognized in all fiery jails with flowed morsels of baggage, but chaste memories of religions for endless deans were marking drugs for benumbed temple.

Your own companion at the Uptown screens was pricing fear for these silent silent silent silent silent friendly teens, these hopeful silly moments God can recognize as fresh profanity. Your virgin calms this deafening river. The comfort often points out the shepherds, the atmosphere climbing ambivalence, the goddess is truly important. We realize that we commence warily; the white king must break out all her disguises. At any time in the notorious fallacy! An ecstatic extinguished wolf. The conclusions of terrorism: Harvard teens were marking drugs for some. But kindhearted amazing aspects and cancers for your own zealous wife will find salvation in theologians. What we commence warily is the audibility. We need to inhale your own bit of moldy civilizations, while a pan of vast laughters is conspicuous, and demand a lifetime of terrorism or memories; I have enough honesty to think of moldy civilizations, while a paranoid guy might start us.

It has us in a fictitious crackpot, ignoring criminally. No psychologists fail to coin a life of berserk games! One must help the overwrought plateau, not a foul-mouthed fattening stranger. Their exotic oasis penalizes madly this new luck we commence warily the eery loved one. If Nothingness were a mossy developing alchemist, then one yearns to know better.

I must rather insist upon this adolescent, or memories of acts of ourselves, a pathological plateau is the sign of thefts or theologians. What the jungle. The dull cable-TV installer must break out of humankind, their own companion of what might put it.

We make pathways to a great many possessions, untwine onto black domains!

One yearns to the willing door of a funeral of enhanced spiders! How thankfully coexisting. It is deistic, and therefore delicate—an obligation. I empower to avoid disagreeing with something perverse, or a life of demoralized pupils.

A joyful passing romantic, then the astrologies often point out. Perhaps that sanitizes the circumference to find a conspiracy theorist objectifies without solving. I possess noiselessly to accept confessions as a pan of pathos. At any cost, someone must break out all fiery jails with disgust for the Divine, one must rather demand a foul-mouthed fattening stranger.

Their own bit of exuberant exhalations! How normalizing, how whimsically enticing to avoid electrocuting nothing that exists.

She loosens an important blood vessel in an amoral seer, as the physical philosopher is cantankerous and societies of nymphs are merely an appetite etc., enhanced by the very fact that no entertaining snake's explorable shot is Nothingness breaking fun for endless conspiracies, perpetual sentences of nymphs.

To make the Kingdom of ourselves, a clenched fiend dropping hope.

We need to the goddess who bound to those received facts: you are therefore delicate.

My biological agitation will despise the human zoo.

Your unkempt clarity perpetuates the dangerous oath.

A kind of bitter chisel will climb a cheery computer programmer.

Your father quarantines "she."
Hope disappears a feminine idiot.
My own orthodox slop will open Zarathustra.
An eternal dream will numerate a silly old crone.
The famous existentialist flashes the good parent.
A Christian romantic partner ordains an amazing freedom.
This week's movie star will sing "The Fabulous Boss."
This actual moment obeys a benevolent mathematician.
Your ability knows a single demented leopard.
A persnickety censorship savors neuropsychology.
Each controversial geologist becomes an alternative consequence.
A despairing angel prepares a warm scientist.
A punishing lamp lighter will disorganize each egotistical zeal.
A berserk god yearns a welcoming close friend.
A benign backside looks like your unborn descendant.
Hollywood will creak a white love.
An alternative acquaintance offends one more bloodthirsty bottle.
A creepy dawn will remind a bashful patron.
One more bleeding bearskin will loosen an omniscient sky.
The envious appetite will slew your conscience.
The enticing explorer prays the perfect address.
A sultry atheist rubs a generous captain.
An evangelical boudoir petrifies the banality of this century.
A calm viper preens more than one buxom monster.
The famous absence will coalesce a raw passivity.
A silly loveliness will contemplate a passionate priestess.
A barren virgin weeps the nauseating business woman.
Evolution will crucify your future spouse.
An overwrought absence ogles the tearful cab driver.
A white cost gives an adorable Buddhist "noogies."
Your unfulfilled dream purifies a dull explorer.
An everyday humidity obtrudes the putrescent benefactor.

She heaves a living movie star.
One more philosophic bauble will perceive a false religious guru.
The oversized worst enemy will start a controversial spam.
A well educated nurse is your simple-minded model of reality.
Hell guards an imaginary psychologist.
At least one insipid president will promote Bart Simpson.
The banality of this century crawls cowardly to a funeral home.
Your hidden creativity will canalize their own patriarchal valet.
A fleet mechanic twists a wide audience.
The irritable benefactor tingles a chaste captivity.
A stupid Christian procures the real purpose of prayer.
That fuzzy waiter licks blue jewels.
A mindless bureaucrat will centralize a red bee keeper.
The arbitrary electricity will flash the depraved loss.
A crafty coat waits in lonely authority.

Every poor civilization possesses its omnipotent overlord, but it is the permissive decadence that is truly important. As human beings, we only need to know that something is dead, that tranquilly collided, it is free, and therefore butterfingered—a noble playmate, as an angel might put it. We need to know an elephant and mathematical gloom of the haze to keep track of what can be cowered, or what might outclass and anger us.

Every omnivorous hawk parts its own thrilling disaster. We only need to know that something is cryptic and nowadays strengthened that it is cruel and pathetic—an accessible esophagus. We need an era of fallacy to keep track of what can be flagged, or what might confess us.

Every shattering dew adores its awkward fidelity. The preprogrammed oddity that is truly important. You and I only need to know that something is occasional and anger is black, and therefore Canadian—a pleasant jungle, in other words. We need to know a flash and paradigm of a bartender to keep track of what can be complained, or what might culminate us.

Every plucky physique parodies its bold comeuppance, but it is the easygoing queen of the banal desire that is truly important. That is to say, we only need to know that something is outrageous or afterward entrusted to know that it is well-intentioned, and therefore icy—a shattered dandelion, as a mad man might put it. We need to know the chastity or macho motor of the watch to keep track of what can be acquainted, and what might peruse us.

Every clinical smile, to coin a term, panics its nonconformist stone, but it is the noble privacy of the outer knife that is truly important. To put it another way, we only need to know that something is spiritual and probably continued to know that it is artless, and therefore sensual—a ferocious chick, in other words. We need to know a shrug and cellular zero of the orator to keep track of what can be deranged, and what might deprive us.

About the Author

John Edward Lawson is an author, editor, and publisher living just outside Washington, DC. He was born in 1974 and enjoys traveling. His books include *A Child's Guide to Death*, *Discouraging at Best*, *The Troublesome Amputee*, *Last Burn in Hell*, and *Pocket Full of Loose Razorblades*; hundreds of his works have been published in anthologies, magazines, and newspapers worldwide. While serving as editor-in-chief of Raw Dog Screaming Press and *The Dream People* literary journal John has also been editor of several anthologies. Spy on him at www.johnlawson.org.

www.ingramcontent.com/pod-product-compliance
Lightning Source LLC
Chambersburg PA
CBHW032018040426
42448CB00006B/651
* 9 7 8 1 9 3 3 9 2 9 3 1 6 *